P9-EGD-022

EX LIBRIS

ARLY TOLETTE

$\mathscr{O}$HOOD $\mathscr{O}$rnaments

Hood Ornaments

Rob Leicester Wagner

MetroBooks

MetroBooks

An Imprint of Friedman/Fairfax Publishers

©2001 by Michael Friedman Publishing Group, Inc.

All rights reserved. No part of this publication may be reproduced, stored in a retrieval system, or transmitted, in any form or by any means, electronic, mechanical, photocopying, recording, or otherwise, without prior written permission from the publisher.

Library of Congress Cataloging-in-Publication Data available upon request.

ISBN 1-58663-090-3

Editor: Ann Kirby
Art Director: Kevin Ullrich
Designer: Wendy Fields
Photo Editor: Lori Epstein
Production Director: Richela Fabian Morgan

Color separations by Fine Arts Repro House Co., Ltd.
Printed in Hong Kong by C&C Offset Printing Co., Ltd.

1 3 5 7 9 10 8 6 4 2

For bulk purchases and special sales, please contact:
Friedman/Fairfax Publishers
Attention: Sales Department
15 West 26th Street
New York, NY 10010
212/685-6610   FAX 212/685-1307

Visit our website:
www.metrobooks.com

Introduction

Famed automotive stylist Virgil Exner always believed that an automobile was just that—an automobile. It consisted of four wheels, an engine compartment, seating for passengers and driver, and a trunk. In Exner's vision, function came first, and form followed. His Chryslers, Plymouths, and DeSotos were known for sculpted beauty based on solid engineering concepts. But his was not the prevailing philosophy of twentieth-century automotive design.

To most others, an automobile, particularly the prewar variety, was never merely a means of transportation—it was also a work of art. And no other aspect of the automobile better denoted artistic merit than the hood ornament, the often elegant, the sometimes gaudy, and the occasionally ridiculous sculpted piece of chrome (or brass, or even crystal) mounted at the top of the radiator, and, with later models on the hood. The hood ornament gave motor vehicles personality, distinction, and above all, sex appeal.

No one better understood this than Harley Earl, General Motors' kingpin of automotive design. Earl began his automotive styling career with the incomparable 1927 LaSalle and ended it in the fin wars between GM and the Chrysler Corporation in the late 1950s. With his famed Art & Colour Section he exercised virtually limitless control over the path taken by General Motors over three decades.

Earl's design department was highly competitive for up-and-coming stylists. During the prewar years and the period immediately following World War II, designers were assigned specific tasks. One might spend a year designing door handles, a trunk lid, or the components of a dashboard. But, oh, the hood ornament—now that was an assignment. That was a task that meant prestige within the rarefied circles of the Art & Colour studio. And the designers of the day were no wallflowers; they were masculine, extroverted men who drank their lunch, caroused with the secretarial staff, and exalted in their manliness. The hood ornaments that they crafted were stamped with their character and personality.

Winged goddesses—those often delicate yet voluptuous wraiths with waist-length hair streaming back and soft-featured faces turned upward—hearkened back to the days of the tall ships, when fair maidens and sirens adorned the vessels of adventurers and pirates. Late '20s Cadillacs featured a fragile female form with backswept arms and a wind-blown gown, a classic Art Nouveau icon known as the Spirit of Ecstasy. Packards of the era were ornamented with a winged woman who held a wheel in her outstretched hands.

But not all hood ornaments had erotic themes. The icon that graced the hood of Hispano-Suizas from 1918 on was designed by Mark Birkigt as an homage to a close friend killed during the First World War. As a memorial to French aviator George Guynemer, who was killed in action in 1917, Birkigt created a flying stork—inspired by the mascot of Guynemer's squadron, whose planes, incidentally, were powered by Hispano-Suiza engines. The flying stork featured a delicate design that was imitated by many other car makers over the decades that followed.

By the early 1930s many automakers had abandoned such sensitive, light styling in favor of Art Deco and Art Moderne motifs. The Bentley Speed Six was festooned with a letter B bisected by a pair of wings. Duesenberg chose a Deco-styled slashed wing. Perhaps the most masculine hood ornament to emerge from the prewar era was the solid neoclassical bust of a winged Greek figure, emphasizing dignity and reliability, on the hood of the Stutz. Bugatti eschewed all pretense of beauty and sublime sensuality by featuring an upright elephant on its radiator cap.

Deco motifs became even more pronounced on the cars built in the years after World War II, especially in the United States. Aircraft designs dominated the hoods of cars from postwar Detroit, with Chevrolet, Pontiac, Oldsmobile, and other automakers adopting winged aircraft or rocket-style ornamentation.

As the influence of Harley Earl waned and more conservative forces began to control automotive styling, the distinct character of individual models began to blur. Boxy styling, flatter hoods, and more streamlined designs made the hood ornament somewhat obsolete. There are, of course, a handful of luxury automakers who have held on to hood ornamentation for decades—the pouncing Jaguar and distinctive Mercedes-Benz badge, for example, remain symbols of prestige and style. But for the majority of automakers, the homogenization of automotive design beginning in the late 1950s spelled doom for the hood ornament. Science and engineering had replaced style and glitz as objects of desire, a change reflected in the almost puritan styling that remains in vogue today.

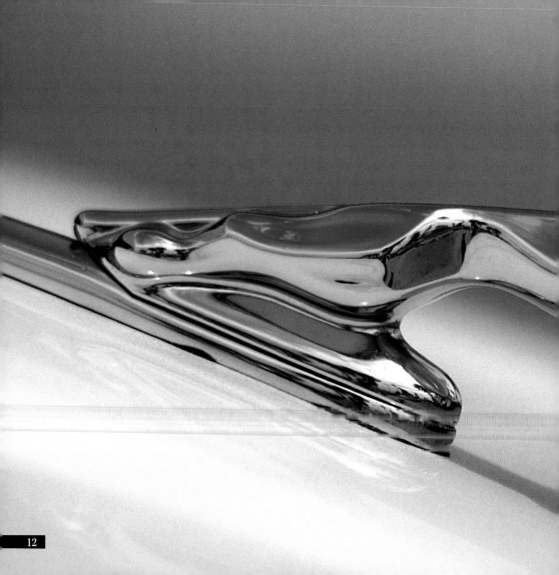

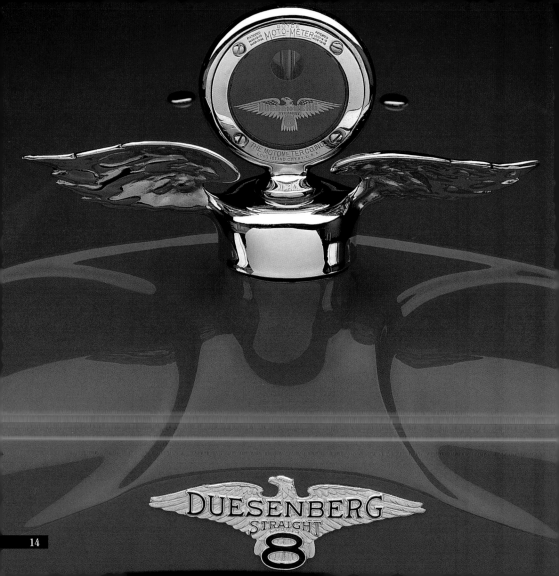

14

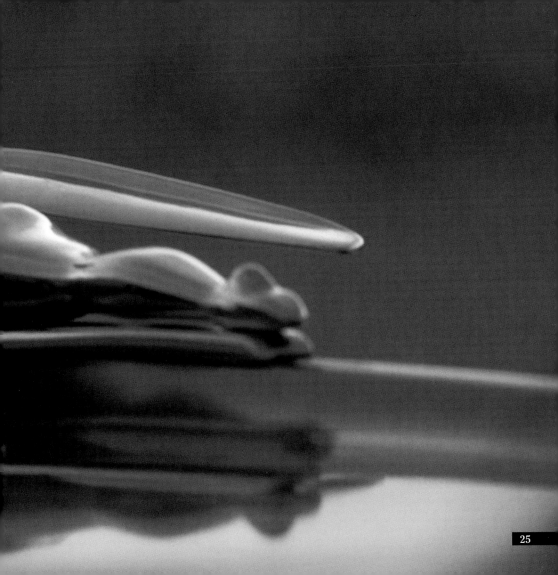

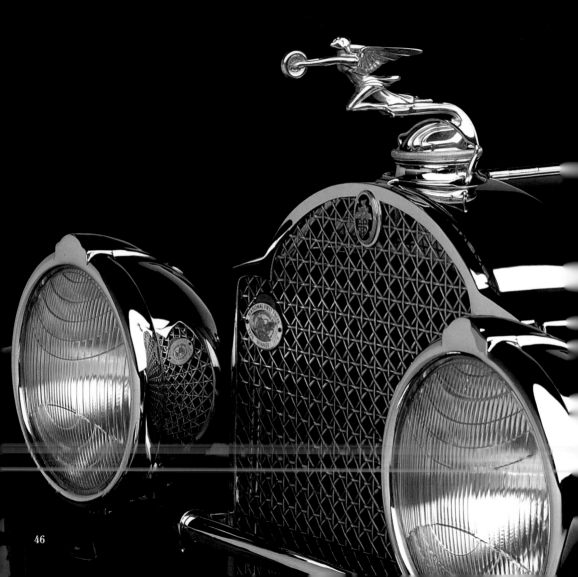

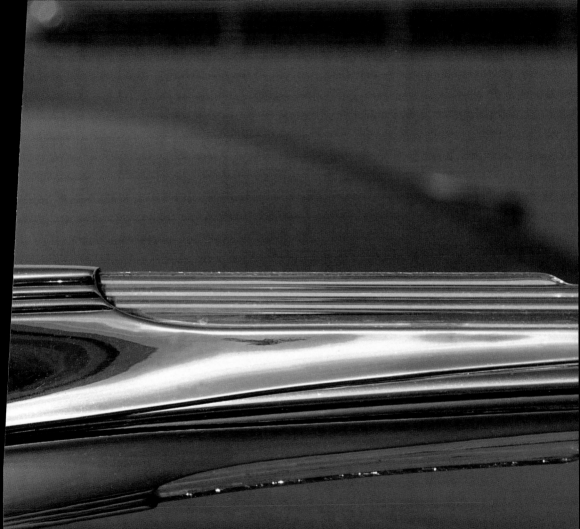

53

60

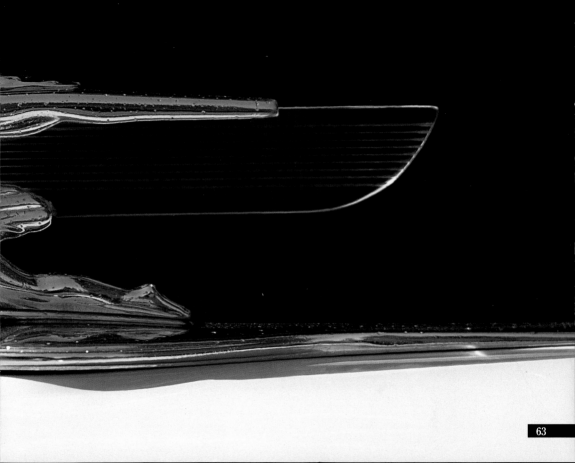

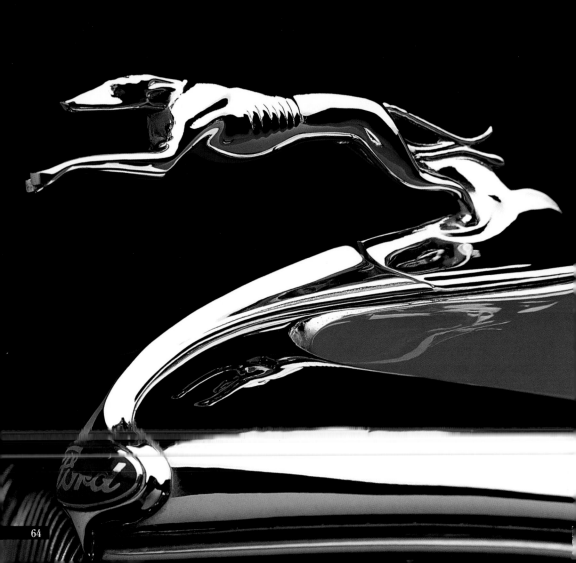

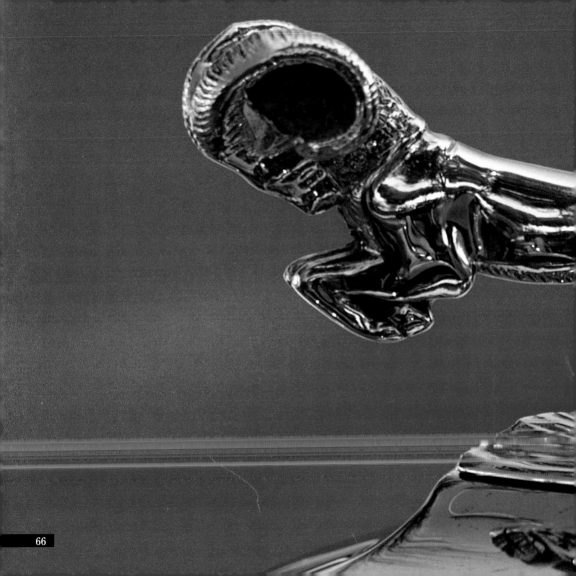

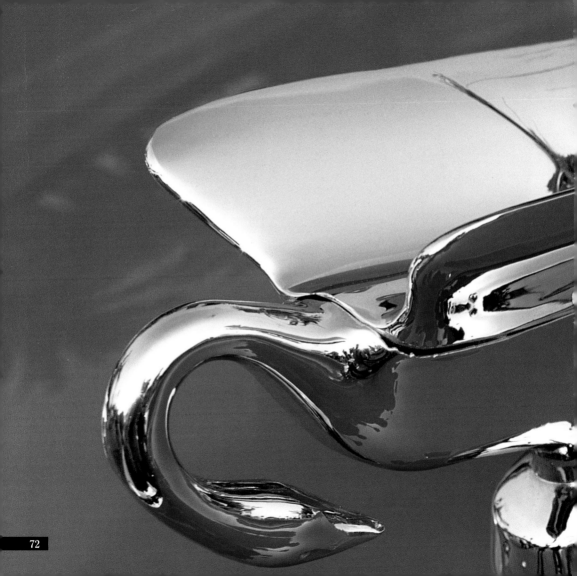

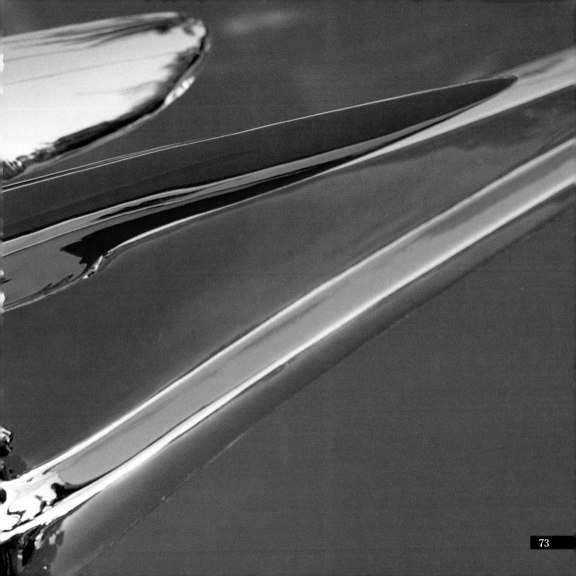

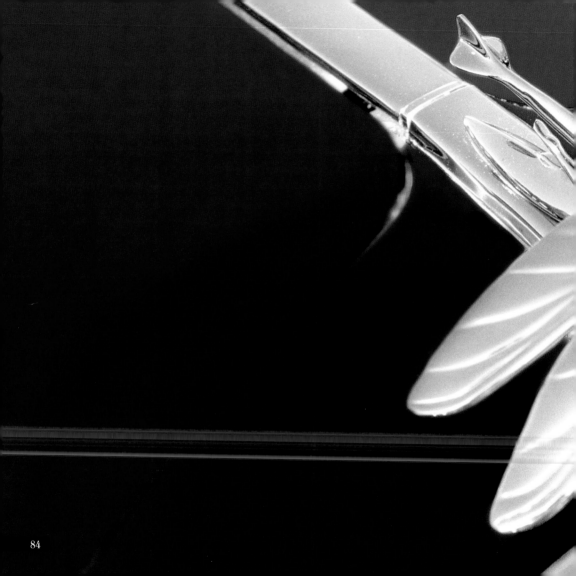

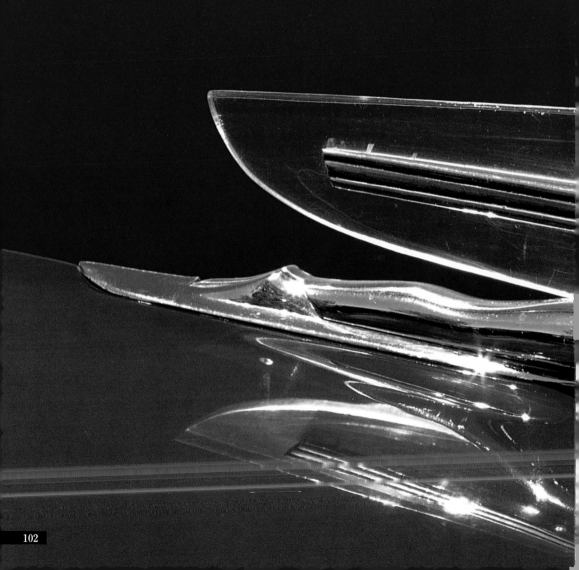

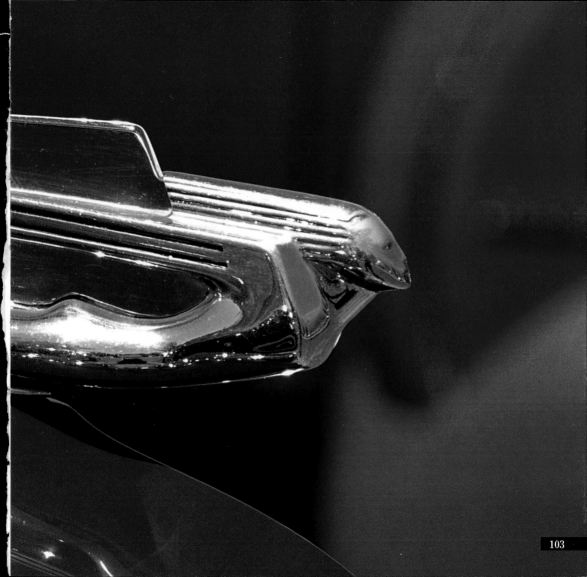

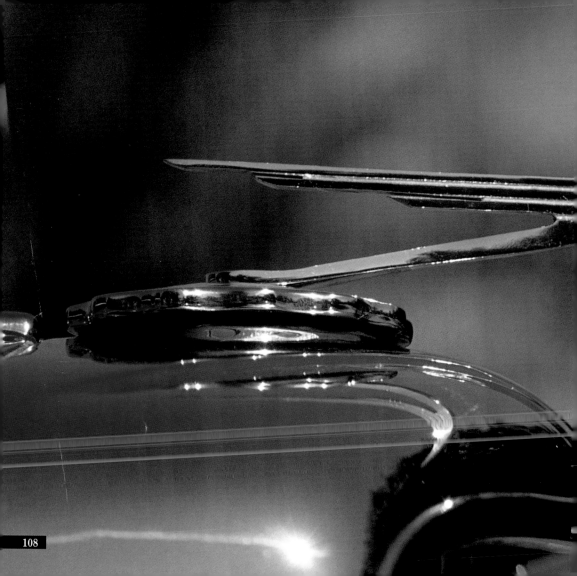

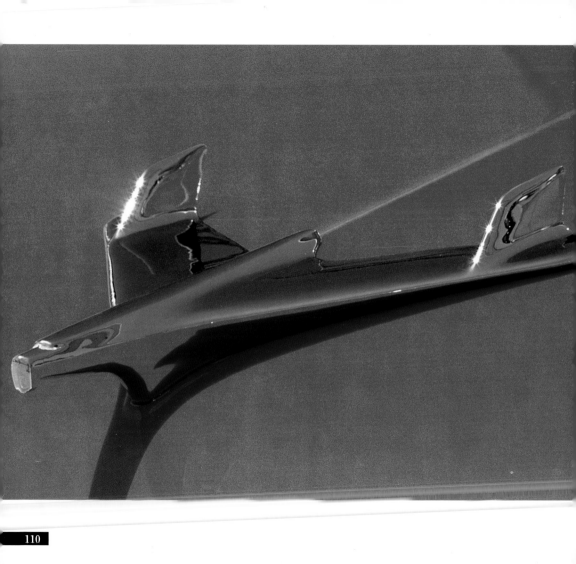

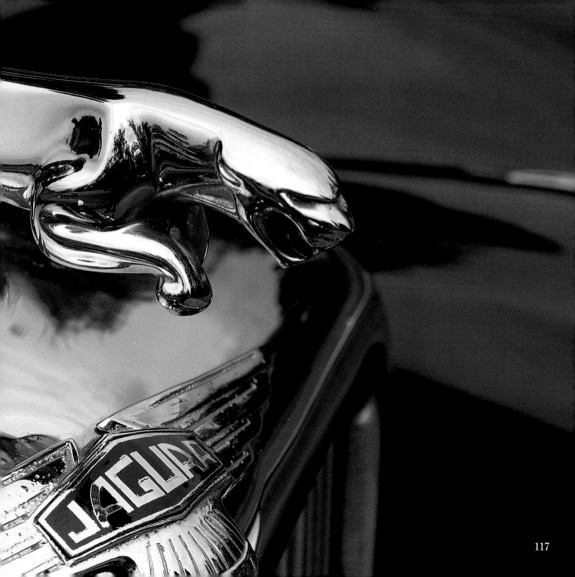

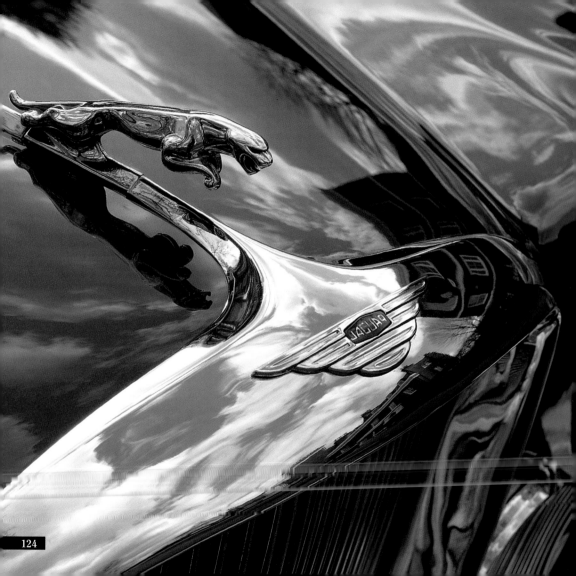

125

Key to Photographs

Publisher's Note: Every attempt has been made to properly identify the mascots and cars included in this collection. However, some of the makes and models were impossible to discern from the photographs provided.

Acknowledgments

Special thanks to Neill Bruce

Photo Credits

©Neill Bruce: 1, 9, 11, 20, 21, 29, 30, 31, 35, 43, 44–45, 47, 48, 49, 53, 58, 62–63, 65, 68, 69, 70, 71, 75, 76, 80, 81, 82, 88, 93, 95, 98, 101, 104, 105, 107, 112, 113, 116–117, 118, 121, 124, 126

©Richard Cummins: 12–13, 16, 27, 28, 36, 37, 40, 55, 61, 66–67, 72–73, 96–97, 99, 110

©Ron Kimball: 2, 5, 8, 10, 14, 18–19, 23, 26, 32–33, 34, 42, 46, 54, 56–57, 60, 64, 77, 78–79, 83, 87, 89, 90–91, 92, 94, 100, 102–103, 106, 111, 115, 120, 125, front endpaper

©Roy Query: 108–109, 114

©Don Spiro: 17, 24–25, 38–39, 50–51, 59, back endpaper

Superstock: 22, 52, 74, 86, 119

©Kat Wolfe: p.15

Zone Five Photo: 122, 123

Zoomstock: 41, 84–85